Library of
Davidson College

Preface by Neil Kinnock MP

KISSINGER'S KINGDOM?

A Counter Report on Central America

by

Stuart Holland MP

Donald Anderson MP

SPOKESMAN

United States distributor
DUFOUR EDITIONS, INC.
Booksellers and Publishers
Chester Springs, PA 19425
215-458-5005

First published in Great Britain in 1984 by Spokesman,
Bertrand Russell House, Gamble Street, Nottingham
NG7 4ET.
Telephone 0602 708318

Second impression 1984

This book is copyright under the Berne Convention. No part of this publication may be reproduced or transmitted in any form or by any means without permission.

Copyright © Spokesman

ISBN 0 85124 403 3

Printed by the Russell Press Ltd., Nottingham

CONTENTS

Preface	i
Introduction	1
Part One - Overview	3
Back Yard and Front Yard	3
The Balkan Analogy	4
Satellite Status	4
The Vietnam Analogy	5
Indirect Intervention - Honduras	5
Direct Intervention? - El Salvador	6
Invasion? - Nicaragua	7
Oligarchy and Dictatorship	8
Pluralism in Question	9
Press Censorship	10
Human and Democratic Rights	11
Civil Defence Committee	12
Economic Freedom	12
The Development Imperative	13
North-South not East-West	14
Part Two - Kissinger and Alternatives	16
De-Stabilisation	16
El Salvador	17
Nicaragua	18
Aid and Arms	19
The Hague Initiative	20
Non Alignment	21
Demilitarisation	22
A New Model of Development	24
Bilateral and Multilateral	25
Part Three - El Salvador	26
The U.S. Embassy	27
Other Diplomatic Opinions	28
Land Reform	29
The Government View	30
Civil Rights	31
The Opposition	33

Part Four - Honduras   35

    Chronic Poverty   35
    Economic Dependence   36
    Economic Crisis   37
    Disappearing Aid   38
    The Government's Response   39
    Democracy in Question   40
    Congress Undermined   40
    Manipulation of the Judiciary   42
    The Armed Forces   42
    Human Rights   44
    Intimidation   45
    Limits to Opposition   45
    Summary   46

Part Five - Nicaragua   48

    Democracy   50
    Elections   50
    Pluralism   51
    Trades Unions   53
    Press Censorship   55
    Miskitos and Others   56
    The Literacy Campaign   58
    The Health Campaign   59
    The Economy   61
    The Cuts in Aid   62
    Military and Milicia   64
    Peace Negotiations   66
    The Nicaraguan Proposals   67

Part 6 - Findings and Recommendations   70

PREFACE BY
THE RT HON NEIL KINNOCK MP
LEADER OF THE LABOUR PARTY

This report results from a fact finding mission which I requested Stuart Holland and Donald Anderson to undertake in Central America in December 1983.

After spending nearly as much time in Central America as the Kissinger Commission and after taking evidence there from a wider range of sources than did that body, they have compiled a document which exposes the flawed reasoning of current US involvement in the region and provides a warning of the dreadful potential of the continued pursuit of present US policy.

As the authors have stressed the problems of Central America are North/South, not East/West. The tensions and instability of the area originate in poverty and exploitation and the great political conflicts arise directly from that source. The United States of America with its immense resources could change the condition of the area but only if its Governments end the historic folly of propping up dependent dictatorships and sabotaging administrations that have been produced by the crisis of under-development. The claim, for instance, that Nicaragua threatens the United States is about as impressive as a report of impending assault by an ant on an elephant. The foreign policy of a Super Power should not be prompted by such paranoia.

Further tragedy can be averted but only if an administration in the United States shows itself to be caring about the problems, constructive in its action and co-operative in its approach. They are the pre-requisites both of the moral authority which the USA needs to gain in its role in international affairs and of the judgement which is specifically required in its view of Central America.

In the USA there is an extensive body of opinion which is opposed to yet another armed crusade against some of the least privileged and most exploited people in the world, the people of Central America. They, like us, will be informed and strengthened by this Report from Stuart Holland and Donald Anderson which in many important ways is a timely and necessary counter to the Kissinger Commission.

Introduction

This report follows a fact-finding mission to El Salvador, Honduras and Nicaragua, leaving London on December 11th, and returning on December 18th 1983. One of us also visited Panama on the return leg of the trip to speak with Salvadoran opposition leaders in exile.

We undertook this visit in our official capacity as Labour front bench spokespersons, on the personal initiative of the Leader of the Labour Party. On our return to Britain we gave a press conference on Tuesday, December 20th which was also attended by Neil Kinnock, who strongly endorsed our preliminary findings. We were well aware that our report might be published at or around the time of the Kissinger Report on Central America. We did not anticipate that our findings would be a counter-report to Kissinger but it is clear that **our analysis and recommendations for the region are fundamentally different from those of the Kissinger Commission.**

Though our visit was brief we note that it was only a day or two less than that of the Kissinger Commission. Our range of contacts and evidence also appears to have been wider. We were able to draw on the experience of those who gave evidence to us and learn directly from a range of people in the various countries – ambassadors and other diplomats, government ministers, politicians – including opposition members in Honduras – from whom the Kissinger Commission apparently took no evidence – journalists, academics, human rights activists, members of the church, non-governmental organisations involved in aid and development programmes – as well as direct interviews with a range of professionals and people themselves. We are grateful to each of them for the time which they spent and consideration they showed to us during the course of our visit. We also were able to benefit from access to a range of documentary evidence in English and Spanish.

Our report includes criticism of structural inadequacies in UK diplomatic representation.

We wish to stress that these judgements in no way reflect upon the integrity of those concerned. In particular we wish to thank Elizabeth Sketchley, Charge d'affaires at the British Embassy in Tegucigalpa, who met us on our arrival in El Salvador, and organised several of our meetings with great courtesy and efficiency. We also are grateful to Peter Summerscale, HM Ambassador in Costa Rica, for meeting us on our arrival in Managua and confirming with us that we were satisfied with the arrangements made independently by us before leaving London.

Not least we are grateful to the representatives of the Catholic Institute for International Relations and of Oxfam working in the region, including those who travelled across Nicaragua to give evidence to us on the background of the question of the Miskito indians. We are impressed by the commitment of these agencies, and their staff, in seeking to help resolve social and economic underprivilege in the area, often under most difficult and hazardous circumstances.

PART ONE - OVERVIEW

It is notorious that several countries of Central America won their independence from Spain in the early 19th century but that following the Spanish-American War of 1898 suffered an endless round of invasion, occupation and intervention by the United States - in Panama, Cuba, Puerto Rico, Honduras, Haiti, Dominica Republic and Nicaragua. All these countries had suffered direct occupation by US troops before 1917 and before the Bolshevik revolution in the Soviet Union. Most of them suffered an action replay thereafter, plus the CIA-backed invasion of Guatemala in 1954.

Back Yard and Front Yard

On these grounds alone it is quite clear that claims made by the United States administration that it needs to intervene in Central America in order to stem Soviet-Cuban aggression is but a new name for an old claim - stemming from the Monroe Doctrine - its self-assumed right to dominate the Central American and Caribbean areas.

For some time it was commonplace to claim that the countries of the region were America's 'back yard'. More recently, the Reagan administration has claimed that 'there is a fire burning in our own front yard', with the associated claims that it is being fuelled and fanned by Cuban and Soviet interests in the area. We find the claim implausible in either geographic, political or military terms. Though it undoubtedly is the case that the Cubans in the 1960's did seek to aid independence movements in Latin America with advisers, direct assistance and arms, they have been notably more cautious in recent years.

In terms of the strategic frontiers between the super powers, Canada is the front yard of the United States and well protected by missile warning systems. In geographic and political terms Mexico is the back yard - sizable, politically stable, and clearly free from Soviet or Cuban influence. Central America is beyond the back yard, and of no military threat to the United States.

The Balkan Analogy

In fact, we are less struck by the front or back yard claims made by the United States than the degree to which **Central America is the Balkans of North America.** As with Balkanisation under the Austro-Hungarian empire, the United States through this century subjected the countries of the region to either indirect dollar diplomacy or direct dealings with dictatorships with appalling records on the suppression of human rights and individual liberties. If anything, its record in the region has been less principled, more self-interested and more repressive than that of the Austro-Hungarian regime in the Balkan countries.

We are surprised that this obvious analogy escaped Henry Kissinger, granted the influence of Metternich and the Austro-Hungarian Empire on his own version of Realpolitik.

Satellite Status

It is clear to us that **Nicaragua today offers no threat to the United States.** Its military force is wholly defensive in character. Consistent with its non-aligned status, Nicaragua has pledged that it will not allow its territory to be used for a military base by either super-power.

In our judgement the threat posed by the Nicaraguan revolution lies more in the extent to which it challenges the United States with a new and autonomous model of social and economic development. **Nicaragua may be a thorn in the underbelly of the Reagan administration, but it is no more so than the thorn in Stalin's side** represented by Yugoslavia after Tito's break with Moscow, while again being more pluralist and democratic in form if not substance than Yugoslavia itself. In making the comparison we are conscious that despite Tito's challenge to Stalinist supremacy, the Soviet Union did not invade Yugoslavia. We submit that if the Reagan administration were to invade Nicaragua it would represent a historic indictment of the United States no less than that of the Soviet Union following the Warsaw Pact invasions of Hungary in 1956 and Czechoslovakia in 1968.

The Vietnam Analogy

It also is clear to us that after a decade in which Vietnamisation has become a dirty word in United States politics, the policies pursued by the Reagan admininstration in Central America are aligning US policy in the region with that which it earlier pursued in Vietnam. In our discussion with American Ambassadors and diplomatic staff in El Salvador, Honduras and Nicaragua, we saw the same symptoms of polarised East-West vision, and the same readiness to support - or subvert - regimes with impunity which characterised early American diplomacy, military aid and intervention in Vietnam.

It nonetheless is clear that there are important differences between the first Vietnam experience in South-East Asia and the second Vietnam which Central America may become. Not least, while Vietnam was and is physically adjacent to the super power of China and explicitly backed by the super power of the Soviet Union, there is no such adjacent or directly-involved 'hostile' super power in the Central American region threatening the interests of the United States. In fact, the adjacent super power in this case is the United States itself which, in our view, for that reason, lacks even the self-justification which it invoked in the case of its earlier and disastrous intervention in Vietnam.

Indirect Intervention - Honduras

In Honduras, paralleling its earlier intervention with military advisers in Vietnam, the United States has already undertaken two major manoeuvres – Big Pine One and Two – building airstrips, training local troops and notoriously giving succour and support to the Contras in their operations in Nicaragua.

These are exercises by occupying forces over which the Honduran government has little or no control. When we asked the Deputy Foreign Minister and two senior Foreign Office officials if they could confirm that Big Pine Three would be in the Ocotepeque region bordering El Salvador and Guatemala they replied 'We don't know yet. The news was only in the papers yesterday'. The Americans are increasingly becoming an occupying power; their Ambassadors pro-consuls and the government – though directly elected – increasingly subject to the army, which itself is subject to Washington.

Direct Intervention? – El Salvador

In El Salvador a well-organised popular army or guerrilla force – the FDR-FMLN – can take almost any territory outside the capital and hold it for some of the time. The 40,000 strong Salvadoran army has only some 8,000 men deployed to fight, and only 2,000 crack troops. These recently have been cracked themselves by the popular army, which late last year retook Cacahuatique in the north-eastern Morazan province (near where Big Pine Three in neighbouring Honduras is scheduled) and recently overran the Salvadoran army garrison at El Paraiso – cutting off a large part of the country from operations by government forces, and their single biggest disaster of the war.

As in Vietnam, neither the notorious death squads – frequently soldiers in 'civvies', countenanced or co-ordinated by the high officer command in the El Salvadoran army – nor bombing of the civilian population as in Tenancingo in September – are gaining hearts or minds. Meanwhile the FDR-FMLN's policy of returning government troops who surrender through the Red Cross both has increased the army's willingness to lay down arms and thereby swelled the guerrilla's arsenals, reducing the need for outside provision. Despite US claims to the contrary, it is striking that no evidence has been produced by them or the Salvadoran authorities that arms from Nicaragua have been provided to the FDR-FMLN.

The situation in El Salvador is so serious that the Americans may well have to intervene directly with ground troops after the forthcoming elections on March 25th - a second main stage in the Vietnamisation of the region. The FDR-FMLN at present do not plan to boycott the elections, despite the fact that no assurances on physical safety - other than behind bars - can be given by the government to opposition politicians.

Invasion? - Nicaragua

It was made clear to us by many individuals whom we met in Nicaragua - although not by government authorities - that following the US invasion of Grenada, a similar invasion of Nicaragua was feared as probable in November. In the back yards of homes, in open space within the 'barrios' we saw slit trenches and shelters dug by the local population in recent weeks under the apprehension of imminent attack. The country is still under alert and in a state of war-readiness, with the milicia wearing uniforms and carrying arms to work. While the threat of such invasion is discounted by the US Ambassador, it is clear that the United States intervened with marines in 1912 and occupied the country until 1925, and thereafter re-occupied the country from 1926 to 1933, with the defeat of Sandino and their establishment of the first Somoza regime with the backing of the National Guard. In our view such a track record more than justifies anxiety on the part of the Nicaraguan people that Nicaragua could shortly be invaded.

The Kissinger Commission claims that it wishes 'to preserve the moral authority of the United States.' But with such a record, plus its evident backing of the Somocista-Contras in their incursions from Honduras, and its warships sailing off both the Caribbean and Pacific coasts, the United States lacks moral authority or justification for its claim that it would not invade Nicaragua. The domestic popularity of the Grenada invasion once successful, could only increase the temptation facing the US administration to intervene.

It is, however, more probable that under pressure coming from domestic public opinion, President Reagan will baulk at the prospect of US troops being directly involved in Honduras, El Salvador and Nicaragua in a pre-election year. **This may take the pressure off Nicaragua in the near future.** The reported CIA evaluation of up to 20,000 US casualties in the event of an invasion of Nicaragua is an undeniable deterrent. Meanwhile, the commitments recently made by the Nicaraguans on the timing of elections; their proposals to the Contadora states for mutual non-aggression and non-intervention should make it more difficult for the US administration to 'legitimate' a Grenada-style invasion allegedly designed to restore democracy.

Oligarchy and Dictatorship

The Reagan administration has suddenly discovered the imperative need for pluralism and democratic elections in Nicaragua. This represents at best the most dramatic conversion since the road to Damascus, and at worst a cynical display of double standards. Having in the first place intervened by force to defeat and overthrow the liberal revolution of Sandino, and established the initial Somoza regime and his National Guard, the United States allowed the use of that so-called guard to terrorise the nation and repress political protest or opposition within the country. **The United States has for decades failed to exert sanctions - similar to those now brought to bear on Nicaragua - against dictatorship and terror squads in Papa Doc's Haiti, dictatorship and official terror in Pinochet's Chile, or military regimes which until recently governed some two-thirds of Latin America's population.**

Similarly, the United States has supported **oligarchy** or rule by a privileged elite - rather than pluralism - in Central and Latin American countries. In El Salvador such oligarchy is illustrated by the claim of rule by fourteen families, in practice an interlinked governing elite. Such political concentration of power has been matched by economic **oligopoly** or control of the economy by a few families and firms. In agriculture, a fraction of the population typically controls a majority of arable land. A handful of United States multinational companies command the processing, manufacturing and agribusiness exports.

Pluralism in Question

Foreign business, domestic dictatorships and direct intervention have dominated the region. They are the reality reflected by US General Smedley Butler accounting his achievements in 1935 as those of a high-class muscleman for big business, Wall Street, and the bankers, making Mexico safe for American oil, Haiti and Cuba a decent place for the National City banks, purifying Nicaragua for the Brown Brothers, bringing light to the Dominican Republic for American sugar interests, and helping make Honduras ripe for the United Fruit Company.

Against such a background it is hardly surprising that any Central American country should face problems in transition to political pluralism. In Nicaragua, the Sandinistas dominate the government and existing political institutions. But it also is clear that they have overwhelming popular support as the leading force in the revolution which overthrew forty-three years of the brutal Somoza regime.

We are no more persuaded than the American Ambassador in Nicaragua that the country is heading towards a one-party state. As he put it 'the scene is more plural than that.'

Nicaragua has established procedures and a timetable for the holding of elections. This followed discussion on electoral procedure. In a country without genuine elections for so long, the delay has been marked, but not wholly indefensible.

We note in passing in this context that it was several years after the ending of hostilities in World War Two that the United States felt the political situation sufficiently stable in Germany and Japan for elections to be held. Nicaragua is still being de-stabilised from abroad.

We also note that had the Sandinistas held a form of elections within the weeks or months immediately following their overthrow of the Somocista regime, they undoubtedly would have received a hegemonic majority. Then rather than now would have been the time for a one-party regime to proceed to a one-party state.

Press Censorship

Much has been made about the issue of press censorship in Nicaragua. We met and discussed the situation with the two brothers who respectively edit the main Sandinista paper (Barricada) and the main opposition paper (La Prensa) while their uncle edits the third main paper (El Nuevo Diario). It was clear from both of them that the vast majority of censored items (up to 85%) concerned military affairs. This covers claims made for Contra incursions into the country, including death and injuries to army, milicia and civilian population, damage, disruption etc. These incursions take place in frontier regions with difficult communications, not least since the Contras in key cases cut communications themselves. It is at least plausible that a country seeking to defend its national security against US-backed incursion from abroad should demand a delay through censorship of the coverage of military affairs.

While undoubtedly other examples of censorship range from over-enthusiastic to the unnecessary and unjustified, **we stress the parallel with two of the world's leading democracies** - the press censorship imposed by the Thatcher government in the United Kingdom during its **Falklands** operations, and the Reagan administration in the US during its invasion of **Grenada.** In the latter case, as the US press, radio and television did not hesitate to stress, journalists were not allowed near the island during the invasion itself, which was entirely reported through official government circles.

We are persuaded that **if Nicaragua were not constantly threatened and actually invaded by the CIA-backed Contras from Honduras, combined domestic and international pressures should be sufficient to lead to a lifting of press censorship.**

Human and Democratic Rights

There are appalling atrocities and thousands of deaths occurring each year in El Salvador. There is a smaller but still considerable number of deaths and disappearances reported annually in Honduras. By contrast, Nicaragua is outstanding in not only the respect which it has shown for the rights of the individual and the due process of trial and justice, but also in its major penal reforms and its policy of rehabilitation.

It is already widely known — though in our view less appreciated than it should be — that **the victory of the Sandinista revolution did not result in revenge killings** of Somocistas or national guards, that **the death penalty was abolished,** that serious efforts at rehabilitation have been made, **and that there are no reports of torture.**

In cases where arrests have been made in areas penetrated by the Contras, on grounds of collusion or support, releases also have been undertaken after a period of detention. We witnessed this — without government prearrangement — in the provincial town of Esteli. We are persuaded that the humanitarian treatment of offenders and the rehabilitation programme are not only real but remarkable in view of the efforts to destabilise the government and the degree to which **the suspension of normal civil liberties while under attack from abroad would** be considered justified in some other countries.

Civil Defence Committees

We are struck by the similar principle but different practice of Civil Defence Committees in Honduras and Nicaragua. Frequently criticised as an importation of a Cuban or Soviet community surveillance system, our findings from direct experience in Nicaragua are that such Watch Committees reflect both local and general public support, and also have a genuine function in a country which is penetrated by Contra incursions. By contrast, Honduras is neither being invaded by government-backed forces from abroad, nor is liable to local subversion from outside forces. Yet its Comites de Defense represent a clear trend towards intimidation and repression of local populations by both the security and armed forces. Insufficient international attention has been paid to the degree to which the so-called Civil Defence Committees in Honduras act in precisely the manner alleged against the local Watch Committees in Nicaragua.

Economic Freedom

We have stressed that in Central American countries such as El Salvador the oligarchy of ruling elites is matched by oligopoly in economic power. In Nicaragua it is again well known - but apparently in some circles of the US administration virtually unrecognised - that nationalisation of property has mainly concerned the former Somoza estates and enterprises. This has raised the share of the public sector in the economy to some 40% of GDP, which is a lower share than in most of the Western European economies and only some two-thirds the size of the public sector in countries such as the Scandinavian countries or the Netherlands. Mass expropriations have not taken place. In cases where land owners quit their properties after the revolution and where ownership has been transferred in their absence, the government has already made it plain that it will pay compensation for the property even where claims have not already been filed.

There is in Nicaragua no attempt to emulate either a Soviet or Eastern European 'command-type' economic system, nor to import the Cuban model. Indeed, several leading figures have publicly stated that they are concerned to learn from the 'mistakes' of Cuban collectivisation. The new and still minoritised model in Nicaragua is of co-operative development rather than state enterprise.

This is combined with a **basic needs** approach to development itself, which in recent years has gained wide international acceptance: i.e. the mobilisation of resources directly to offset malnutrition, open and disguised unemployment, lack of medical and health care, housing and sanitation etc, rather than a strategy based on **trickle-down** effects from income and wealth generated through the export sector or export-dependency.

The remarkable success of this basic needs approach in Nicaragua within a very short period of time contrasts markedly with neighbouring Honduras. Indeed, **it may be because Nicaragua has achieved so much, with so little in so short a time that it has posed a threat to vested interests in the United States.**

Certainly the fact that the basic needs approach contrasts markedly with President Reagan's own trickle-down approach in domestic policy has not gone unnoticed. Nor has the degree to which possibly the main threat to the United States interest in the Central American area is represented precisely by this new, increasingly self-managed and autonomous model of economic development rather than dependence on the export outlets of US multinational capital or foreign aid through US-funded agencies.

The Development Imperative

In our view, however irritating such a challenge may be to either the Reagan administration itself or the United States, there is no justification for the virtual abolition of the sugar import quota by the US authorities, nor in the cutting of aid programmes after the initial period in which already committed resources were disbursed by international aid agencies. Nicaragua suffers from a per capita income level among the very lowest and least developed in the world - comparable with those of Chad, Niger, Mali, Upper Volta or Bangladesh. Such petulant and politically-motivated reduction of the aid programme by the United States is an indictment of the US administration, and its diminished moral authority. The cuts in aid and trade have reduced the living standards of some of the already poorest people in any country anywhere in the third world.

There is indeed a profound struggle for power in this area of extreme poverty and massive international indebtedness. All countries depend on a narrow range of agricultural products where world price has declined. All have been hit hard by the increase in petrol prices. From all there has been a flight of capital. The Central American debt excluding Mexico is in excess of $14 billion. There is scant chance of paying even the interest. In many ways the region's economies are complementary. Yet this interdependence cannot be matched by policy co-ordination because of political differences. In most countries necessary reforms are blocked by coalitions who benefit from the maldistributioon of power and resources.

North-South not East-West

It is clear that the American discovery of the importance of human rights, land reform and democratic elections in Central America follows directly from the success of the Sandinista revolution in Nicaragua. For decades - with the major exception of the earlier years of the Carter administration - the US has neglected such issues in Central or Latin America.

Demanding land reform today in El Salvador, it has no development programme for Honduras and has cut both aid and trade quotas with Nicaragua. Pressing for rights, it still subsidises the Salvadoran regime and plans to double military aid to El Salvador. **Obsessed with claims of Soviet-Cuban destabilisation, the United States refuses to recognise that the problems of Central America are North-South not East-West.** Regrettably, it seems clear that the US administration will subordinate any issue - including land reform, amnesties, or elections - to its strategy of counter-insurgency in the region. It is the United States - not Cuba, nor the Soviet Union - which should be pressured from Europe as well as the Americas to withdraw its military intervention from the Central American region.

PART TWO - KISSINGER AND ALTERNATIVES

De-Stabilisation

The Kissinger Commission warns that the Soviet Union is threatening 'a strategic coup of major proportions' in Central America. By contrast, we find no evidence whatever for the claim that the Soviet Union is significantly involved in the region. Moreover, in this respect we find the Kissinger Commission self-contradictory inasmuch as it recognises in its chapter on security issues that the revolutionary change in Central America is indigenous in nature and not in itself 'a security concern of the United States.'

For this reason we find it the more remarkable that the Report also claims that 'the concerting of Soviet and Cuban power to extend the influence and expand the presence of those nations in vulnerable areas of the Western hemisphere is a direct threat to US security interests.' We also are sceptical of the claim that 'a critical factor in the ability of the United States to sustain a tolerable balance of power on the global scene at a manageable cost has been the inherent security of its land borders, which have not required frontier defences'.

At present there are a few outmoded T54 tanks in Nicaragua, separated by Honduras, El Salvador, Guatemala and the vast land mass of Mexico from the US border. The Nicaraguans have no supersonic aircraft to our knowledge, a handful of sub-sonic aircraft and derisorily few helicopters. Also, any part of the United States is closer to nuclear attack from submarine-launched missiles than it would be from missiles located in Nicaragua. The security claims of the Kissinger Commission of threat to the borders of the United States from Nicaragua themselves cross the borders of fantasy.

We have already argued that there is no

evidence that Nicaragua is a satellite state of the Soviet Union. **If the satellite analogy is to be pursued, Central America as a whole is a satellite region of the United States.**

The Kissinger Report claims that 'from the standpoint of the Soviet Union, it would be a strategic coup of major proportions to impose on the United States the burden of landward defences .. if they succeeded in doing so, they would have out-manoeuvred us on a global scale.' **This is simply alarmist.** There is no evidence to date of any military threat from Central America towards the United States, nor any clear likelihood of such a threat in the indefinite future.

El Salvador

The Kissinger Report recommends as much as $400 million in additional military funds for El Salvador over the two years 1984-1985. This implies not only an increase from some $80 millions to $160 millions for fiscal 1984, as indicated to us by Ambassador Pickering in El Salvador, but a further increase to $240 million in fiscal 1985 - in other words a very marked escalation of military aid.

We understand the reasons why the Kissinger Report claims that 'in a guerrilla war, a stalemate is not the same as a balance of power. It is in the nature of such a war that the insurgency is winning if it is not losing, and the government is losing if it is not winning'. Similar points were made to us during our visit to El Salvador from various sources.

However, we regret to note that the Kissinger solution to the problems in El Salvador is essentially military, and directly paralleled by US strategy in Vietnam, that is - (1) an increase in the Salvadoran army and the training of units capable of more flexibility and greater fire power; (2) increased air and ground mobility to reinforce ambushed troops and counter guerrilla activity; (3) a 'much larger' stock of equipment and supplies; (4) improved medical evacuation to reduce the fatality rate and; (5) funds to permit the Salvadoran army to retain trained personnel for additional tours of duty.

While El Salvador is in geographical terms a small and compact country rather unlike Vietnam, and while through both troop displacement and exercises such as Big Pine the United States in effect already controls the Vietnamese 'hinterland' equivalent of Laos and Cambodia we are not persuaded that a military solution can resolve the problems of El Salvador. Nor are we persuaded that the Salvadoran army will be able decisively to defeat the Front forces without aligning itself increasingly with d'Aubuisson's ARENA Party and that section of the Salvadoran army which is directly or indirectly implicated with the death squads.

Nicaragua

The Kissinger Report claims that the Sandinista revolution in Nicaragua in 1979 was 'a decisive event' in terms of Communist expansion, matched only by the accession of Fidel Castro to power in Cuba in 1959. We have already indicated why we consider this to be a false analysis. However, if taken seriously by the Reagan administration, it also could prove a fatal error of judgement for the United States in Central America, Latin America and before world opinion. In mediaeval France the Manichaeans were pilloried for their bipolar view of the world into good and evil, saved and unregenerate. It has been commonplace for some time that the President of the United States shares the simplism of the Manichaeans - modishly expressed in Star Wars rhetoric. It is disappointing to find that a Commission chaired by as subtle a man as Henry Kissinger also has succumbed to this view. We are struck by press reports on divisions within the Kissinger Commission, and by the claim of one Democratic participant that the compromise on this aspect of the Report had been based on the assumption that 'you (the Democrats) give him the garbage and we (the Republicans) will change the policy'. By achieving a largely consensus report this loyal Republican has done a worthy job for his President in an election year.

We certainly admit that there are parallels between the revolutions in Cuba and Nicaragua, but not those stressed by the Kissinger Commission. First, both revolutions were popularly-based, and achieved by overwhelming odds under the leadership of groups which were essentially national independent. Second, both such revolutions succeeded essentially because of the tyrannies to which they were opposed and the lack of any alternative parliamentary or democratic means of displacing them. Third, both revolutions were in large part anti-American, essentially because of that dual combination of internal oligarchy and external oligopoly - or the liaison between dictators and dollars - which we have already stressed.

The striking feature of the Cuban revolution which surely should be clear to Henry Kissinger is the extent to which an independent nationalist was forced into the arms of the Soviet Union by the embargo on trade and the cutting of aid from the United States. We find it at best surprising and at worst incredible that Henry Kissinger cannot be aware of the parallel in this respect with Nicaragua. In this case the analysis of the Kissinger Commission - though in our view currently without foundation - could become self-fulfilling.

Aid and Arms

We note with grave concern that the Kissinger Commission calls for the repeal of the 1974 legislation in the Foreign Assistance Act barring the use of US aid for the training or support of police forces, and also for the prohibitions on US support for internal surveillance activity.

We note that the report calls overall for an increase of United States aid to Central America of $8 billions by 1990 and up to $24 billions long-term. The Commission advocates that some half of that total should be supplied by the World Bank, International Monetary Fund and the Inter-American Development Bank, plus private investment and commercial banks. We find it difficult to accept that such aid can be conceived as genuinely multilateral rather than indirectly bilateral.

We are sceptical both of the scale of aid and of its intent. When the Commission's report itself is essentially concerned with strategic and military issues, we note that it is cautious on the link between increased military aid and human rights. In the case of El Salvador, we also note that it includes as a basic condition the need for the Salvadoran army to be able to 'carry out US-style counter-insurgency'.

We not only regret the lack of vision of the Kissinger Report. We also regret its amnesia. If it once was said that history repeats itself first as tragedy and then as farce, we regret to say that in the case of the Kissinger Commission, after all the transparent lessons of Vietnam, it is set to repeat itself again as tragedy.

The Hague Initiative

In contrast with our disappointment at disagreement with the findings of the Kissinger Commission, we are impressed by the recommendations of the conference involving North Americans, Central Americans and Europeans held in The Hague from 6th-25th June 1983.*
Important keynote addresses were given to this conference by both Joop den Uyl, former Prime Minister of the Netherlands and present leader of the Dutch Labour Party, and O.R. Carazo, former President of Costa Rica and present Chancellor of the United Nations University for Peace.

---
*(An Alternative Policy for Central America and the Caribbean, The Hague, INEAS (Instituto de Investigaciones Economicas y Sociales) and CRIES (Coordinadora Regional de Investigaciones Economicas y Sociales).

The Hague initiative makes three important recommendations: (1) non-alignment (2) demilitarisation, and (3) a new or alternative model of economic development.

It stresses that, for this to be viable, fundamental social and economic changes must be achieved in the countries themselves, corresponding to majority needs, and not, as at present, reinforcing minority privileges.

We do not underestimate the challenge of these proposals. Nor do we neglect that they raise questions as well as provide answers. For instance, is demilitarisation feasible, and how could it be achieved? What would be meant by a genuine non-alignment rather than the nominal non-alignment of some states elsewhere? What would be meant in practice by a new or alternative model of economic development?

Non-Alignment

Achieving non-alignment lies in part in the perception of the countries of Central America, but also in those of the super powers. We comment elsewhere in this report on what may have been initial expectations of both Nicaraguans and Cubans from the Sandinista revolution. We claim that while it may well have been the case that the Nicaraguan government was interested in supporting - and possibly exporting - revolutions in other countries through assistance with arms (on which we have no direct evidence) it certainly appears clear now - not least in the mutual security and non-subversion treaties proposed officially by Nicaragua within Contadora in December 1983 - that the Sandinista government is serious about agreement on mutual non-subversion of countries in the region.

Regarding Honduras, although it was claimed to us by the Deputy Foreign Minister that the government in Tegucigalpa that his government does not support the Contra's bases in his country, it is widely recognised that in reality the Contras are dependent for their major armed incursions into Nicaragua on the support of the

Honduran government. But that government in Tegucigalpa, in turn, is acting as an agent for the United States through the Big Pine manoeuvres, exercises, and training. The United States may well intervene in El Salvador with ground troops following the elections on March 25th. By contrast, neither Cuba nor the Soviet Union have ground troops deployed on manoeuvres, nor is there evidence that they have made available even ground-to-air defence missiles to the Sandinistas in Nicaragua.

It is clear that the challenge for non-alignment in Central America is posed primarily to Washington rather than Moscow. In the longer term, we are not entirely pessimistic about the prospects. There is a wide section of opinion in the United States which is sensitive to the dangers of super power East-West politics played in the region. We regret that the Reagan administration and the Kissinger Commission appear incapable of recognising the advantage to the security of the United States from a genuinely non-aligned Central American region. Granted not least the criticisms recently made by Dr Kissinger of Western European 'neutralists' who suddenly refused to see the world through American eyes, we urge European governments, parties and public opinion to stress the importance of non-alignment in the region on both the US authorities and on US public opinion.

Demilitarisation

Both the Kissinger Commission and the earlier Caribbean Basin Initiative launched by President Reagan in February 1982 characterised popular struggles in the Central American region as the result of external subversion. We share the judgement of the Hague Declaration that this obscures the fact that **growing militarisation of the region results in good measure from the inflow of arms and equipment provided by the United States itself.**

Of course, arms supplies by the United States to the countries within the region are not new. However, whereas previously they have in the main been supplied to governments on grounds of self-defence (though in practice used mainly to intimidate and repress local population) a major change in US policy is occurring with its support for the Contras incursion into Nicaragua.

In view of the new security agreements proposed by the Sandinista government in Nicaragua for mutual non-aggression and non-subversion within the region, plus a phased reduction of arms, and confidence-building measures between countries, **demilitarisation is in our view a feasible strategy which should be backed to the full by the United States.** The possibility is illustrated by the fact that Costa Rica has no standing army rather than a local police force.

We recognise the improbability that a United States administration, even in the longer-term, would be prepared to include Panama in such a demilitarised perspective, granted its extensive number of bases in the region. We do not regard mutual **abolition** - rather than **reduction** - of defence forces as feasible in the medium to long term in the region.

However, indigenous military forces in the region (with the exception of the Contras) are de facto defensive rather than offensive. We have illustrated elsewhere in this report the extent to which, for instance, the Sandinista government in Nicaragua lacks any supersonic fighter or fighter-bomber aircraft, or modern tanks, in contrast with the materiel of Honduran armed forces, and the degree to which claims of a Nicaraguan offensive capacity is overstated by inclusion by United States authorities of those carrying arms in the milicia as a Nicaraguan 'army'.

We are persuaded that with due agreement for mutual supervision, there is no reason why progress towards demilitarisation in the region should not be achieved. Again, within the context of progressive non-alignment, the supervision of such demilitarisation could appropriately be undertaken by the United

Nations.

A New Model of Development

The Concept of a new model of development is argued in some detail by the summary and conclusions of the Hague Conference of June 1983, and we strongly support its recommendation that 'the need to formulate a new style of development and a new democratic economic model is at the very heart of an alternative regional project'.

The Hague declaration stresses that **satisfying the basic needs of the impoverished majorities** is paramount, — in the areas of food, housing and clothing as well as in the sphere of health and education. We also support the Hague recommendation that the export markets of the Central American countries should be diversified to reduce dependence on one main export outlet (i.e. the United States) and draw the attention of Western European governments to this.

In contrast with the poorest economies in the world with whom some of the countries of the Central American region directly compare in terms of GDP per head, the region in fact includes some of the world's best land and resources. The economic problems of the region stem essentially from its dependent underdevelopment and its maldistribution of internal resources.

We again recommend the economic strategy of the Hague Declaration including a **mixed economy** which would combine:

(1) **a public sector exercising strategic control over foreign trade and finance;**

(2) **a rural and urban sector pioneering new forms of cooperative and municipal enterprise** (not unlike that now being prototyped in various Western European countries through local enterprise agencies);

(3) **a modern private sector, continuing to play a key role,** though focussing attention

on the promotion of small and medium-size enterprise and the provision of financial incentives.

Bilateral and Multilateral

We stress that there are major international constraints on the achievement of such a model of autonomous development focussed on **basic needs** and a **mixed economy,** not least the 'conditionality' of IMF and other multilateral aid. In the case of IMF lending, such conditionality amounts to the combined recommendations of (1) deflation of public spending to 'release resource for export'; and (2) devaluation to 'improve competitiveness in foreign trade'.

We also note that the Kissinger Commission is imposing a new form of political-economic 'conditionality', in effect demanding both political and military alignment with the strategic interests of the United States as a condition of economic aid.

We are convinced that such economic conditions, designed to impose financial rigour on the countries concerned, in reality threaten **rigor mortis** for their economies, as in Costa Rica.

PART THREE - EL SALVADOR

We had a chilling introduction to this war-torn country - driven from the airport in an official car which had what appeared to be a bullet hole by the head of the rear-seat passenger. The chauffeur then drove us backwards up the fast lane of a dual carriageway to avoid a procession in honour of the Order of the Virgin of Guadeloupe. Leaving our hotel, three men left a dark-windowed Chevrolet estate wagon armed with sub-machine guns, rushed past us. Naturally, we were glad to find that they were on routine business. Certainly violence is transparent in downtown San Salvador.

We arrived just after a speech by Vice President Bush in which he had warned the Salvadoran leadership that they put in jeopardy the support of US public opinion so long as they failed to deal with the right-wing death squads. This was a speech more in exasperation than anger by a quasi-colonial ruler unable to enforce its policies. Significantly d'Aubuisson, President of the Constituent Assembly and Presidential candidate of ARENA had boycotted the speech. Once described by the US embassy as a 'pathological killer', he illustrates the difficulty for the United States in giving assurances that continued military and economic aid will be matched by effective pressure on human rights.

Last year more than 5,000 people, most allegedly leftist sympathisers or simply peasants filing land reform claims, were murdered or just disappeared. It was generally accepted that the vast majority of the atrocities were on the government side; indeed the FDR-FMLN had recently treated captured government troops so well that they were considered potentially unreliable on their release through Red Cross agencies.

Ambassador Tom Pickering, a well-meaning man, probably is well aware that the two key US officials in charge of intervention in Central America, Assistant Secretary of State Thomas

Enders and Ambassador Dean Hinton, had been dismissed as being too soft on the anti-communist crusade. He had been careful to clear with Washington his description of the death squads as 'fascists serving the cause of communism'.

The US Embassy

Sitting with Ambassador Tom Pickering in the high-walled, well-armoured and sumptuous US Residence - reminscent of a Fellini film set - we could have been with the United States Ambassador in Saigon a year or so before the Final Days. According to the Ambassador the crack troops were performing well, there was limited popular support for the FDR-FMLN Front forces, and land reform was on schedule.

With an author's enthusiasm Ambassador Pickering told us of four demands which he was pressing on the El Salvador government including: (1) that progress should be made with the arrest and trial of those involved in the murder of the American nuns, where he said that he expected a conviction by March; (2) procedures for the election timetable (anticipated for the 25th March); (3) due procedures for arrest and trial, rather than arrest, detention, and disappearance; (4) a special investigation into the death squads.

Some progress may be made in some of these areas. For instance, it was reported on Monday January 9th 1984, that El Salvador's President Alvaro Magana plans to exile three military officers for allegedly running death squads, and also to create a commission composed of military men to investigate death squad activity.

However, in the same report it appears that President Magana admitted that he is 'having trouble finding the people willing to serve' on the death squad commissions. Further, it is not clear that the US administration will be able to gain effective leadership or arraign presidential candidate d'Aubuisson, previously reported in the New York Times as having asked senior army officers who would rid him of the troublesome - and later murdered - Archbishop Romero. If the United States makes progress with some of the branches of the death squad problem, tackling the roots would displace precisely that part of the high command of the army which the FDR-FMLN is demanding be dismissed as a precondition of negotiations.

We have already reported on the major setbacks for the armed forces which have occurred since our visit, and the apparent breaking of the previous military stalemate.

We were assured by Ambassador Pickering that the United States intended to double military aid to San Salvador (from approximately $80 million to $160 million) but it was not clear to us in what way this could or would be related to the pressures for internal reforms.

The US Embassy in San Salvador lives in a looking-glass world. It is clear that the United States would be glad to bring pressure to bear for effective action on human and civil rights - not least in the question bringing the murderers of the nuns to trial. However it is not clear that they can exact pressure through withdrawal or reduction of aid to achieve this result. It was reported to us from various sources that ARENA presidential candidate d'Aubuisson would be glad for the Americans to withdraw so that his hands could be untied for an all-out confrontation with what he considers to be 'the Communist menace'. **The rhetoric which the Reagan administration has been employing perversely legitimates the arguments of d'Aubuisson among his own supporters.** The Americans appear to will the end of 'smashing the menace' while being unwilling to let local fascists get on with the job.

Other Diplomatic Opinions

Our conviction that the US Embassy was out of touch was confirmed by discussions which we had with other diplomatic representatives in El Salvador. As against the US Embassy's assumption that two crack battalions could 'do the job' in containing the popular forces (a point of view echoed by the Kissinger Commission which recommends increasing military aid to allow the creation of a special rapid reaction force of a 1,000 men) other diplomats put to us the point that while the government already has some 40,000 men in the Salvadoran army, most of these are on garrison or desk duty, with only 8,000 front line troops, matching the 8,000 force which can be deployed by the Front forces. In their view, the army could in due course retake any area occupied by the guerrillas, but not hold it. The more recent events with the Front's taking of the area around El Paraiso, and cutting road/bridge and other communications links with its hinterland certainly appear to have moved the advantage in the short term decisively in favour of the Front and to have broken even the previous degree of stalemate in relative military strength between the respective forces.

Land Reform

It also was put to us by other diplomatic sources that the emphasis on **land reform** made by the United States administration - with its carefully articulated three main phases - is **politically meaningful** inasmuch as it may have dissuaded up to half the Salvadoran peasantry from going over openly to the FDR-FMLN, but is **economically meaningless** - both because land reform has no meaning during a civil war, and also because of the nature of the reform proposals themselves.

The former point seems well made. It is clear that a high proportion of those executed in barbaric manner by the death squads have been campesinos or peasants who have had the courage to file land claims under the first and third parts of the reform programme already passed. During our stay in San Salvador the Assembly refused to pass the bizarrely mis-named second phase of the land reform programme concerning medium-sized properties.

It is clear from the contrast in the concern of the US authorities with land reform in El Salvador, and their total lack of either a land reform or development programme for Honduras, that the United States has pressed for reforms with the intention of undermining the political base of the FDR-FMLN. While it also is clear that this may have had some political effect in the short term, we agree with the judgement that in economic terms the land reform is meaningless, and currently a shambles.

The Government View

We met and talked at length with the Deputy Foreign Minister of Honduras, who claimed to us that the 'rebel forces' only can hold some twentieth of the country. He also alleged that the death squads 'do no more damage than the guerrillas'. On the murder of the nuns, he claimed that six men had been charged a year ago, and that the trial would take place during February and March.

The four main conditions of the FDR-FMLN for cessation of hostilities include (1) power sharing in government, (2) reforms of the army and shared power with the military, (3) negotiations before elections and (4) the resignation of President Mangana (only appointed, not elected). The Deputy Foreign Minister made plain to us that these conditions were unacceptable. On the other hand it clear to us that in government circles there is a real fear that d'Aubuisson and ARENA would win elections in March and that if they do, there is a real fear for the future of the country.

From our talks not only with the Deputy Foreign Minister but also with others in San Salvador it seems clear to us that **the Americans realise that the government has no real power.** The situation in the country is polarised between the FDR-FMLN on the one hand and ARENA on the other. One of the critical weaknesses of US policy is precisely that they seek a centre ground compromise or consensus, when no such independent or neutral centre ground exists.

Civil Rights

We took evidence on the civil rights situation in El Salvador during our visit from unofficial sources. It was reported to us that **there had been as many as 5,400 killings overall in the period from January to October 1983**, with some 1,500 persons killed by the death squads. It was stressed to us that the problem is not just the death squads alone, but also the army and the civil guard. It also was pointed out to us that since September 1983 the death squads have been prepared to publish their activities for the first time.

Apart from the appalling loss of life, some 840 persons had been arrested by them between January and October. In addition to this 544 persons were known to be missing. The polarisation of forces to is increasing rather than decreasing.

While there is a jury system in El Salvador, it was put to us by independent sources that the system simply does not work (1) through intimidation and murder, (2) because decree 507 of the constitution does not automatically allow the right of a defence lawyer, (3) the same decree also allows conviction on confession under torture, (4) the civil legal system is corrupt and (5) does not cover political cases. In words stated as bluntly to us 'with the present legal system, **everything the army wants, the army gets.**' It also was submitted to us that 'the violation of human rights is essential to this government to suppress opinion.'

On the other side, it also was claimed that from January to October there had been 37 kidnappings and 67 killings 'from the Left'. While clearly unacceptable, there is a marked contrast between these numbers and those now claimed outright by the death squads, or widely attributed to the army and the civil guard. Moreover, it also was submitted to us that there has **not been a single claim of torture from the Left**, whereas all the cases taken to the Mariona prison had involved reports of torture as well as those to the Carcel de Mujeres, which in addition had involved reports of both torture and rape.

It was in these informal discussions that we heard the plausible claim that an arbitrary division could not be made between the death squads, paramilitary and army groups since the same groups 'changed their clothes' for different operations. Also, while many lawyers with considerable courage will take up civil rights cases, others refuse to do so granted the fear of reprisals. In the case of the murder of Archbishop Romero, the judge first received a death threat and then 'disappeared'. In other cases, judges who have issued orders to release prisoners have been ignored by the High Court, and arrested persons remain uncharged, violating even the new special law introduced allegedly to remedy this situation.

Within the category of human rights, we also gained independent evidence on the army bombing of Tenancingo in September 1983, where the army bombed the town after it was taken by Front forces. It was submitted to us that this occurred despite the fact that the Green Cross put up white flags, and that it was quite evident that military forces were not in the area being bombed. After the bombing the FDR-FMLN released a tape recording which it was claimed had been gained as a transcript from a recorded conversation between one of the pilots of the bombing aircraft and the ground commander. Allegedly the pilot stated 'how can I bomb - these are civilians?' and the ground commander replied 'everything that moves is enemy.' It is reported that 75 civilians were killed in the bombing of Tenancingo, including three Green Cross volunteers.

The suspension of human rights and civil liberties has not excluded the church. Apart from the scandalous murder of Archibishop Romero and of the American nuns, it was claimed to us that eleven priests have been assassinated in El Salvador and 'literally hundreds of catechists, lay preachers etc'. In 1980 a residence of Jesuit priests was twice bombed and machine-gunned. More recently a bomb exploded in the residence, which then was subjected to an 11-hour search. As one of those involved said: 'if this happens to Jesuit priests you can imagine what happens to the simple peasant'.

The Opposition

Meeting the opposition within El Salvador is understandably difficult since most of them are with the FDR-FMLN forces. It was partly because of this that one of us travelled on the last leg of our visit to Panama for a meeting with Guillermo Manuel Ungo, Secretary-General of the Democratic Socialist MNR, and a Vice-President of the Socialist International.

On the question of the death squads Ungo claims that these are not independent of the government, and that there is a structural and functional linkage between both. He made what seems to us the important point that repression varies in intensity, and at the moment it is directed against those willing to enter negotiations or have talks. As he put it **'these murders are specific messages. Talks are a dirty word, and anyone linked with them is under a death sentence.'** Ungo stressed that finishing the activities of the death squads was not a technical or tactical matter. It would need a change in the structure of power and a new government.

On elections and negotiations Ungo claimed that the United States and Salvadoran governments are posing a false dilemma, i.e. elections **against** negotiations. In contrast, he claimed that the FDR-FMLN were not opposed in principle to elections, and this has been confirmed since our visit by the statement and reports in the international press in January 1984. What he stressed amounted to the difference between the form and substance of elections, posing the question — in a situation of terror in which any citizen suspected of being in opposition is liable to be killed, jailed or to disappear — whether elections can be said to be free.

Ungo claimed that the MNR are not looking for a military victory and that no one wants a prolonged war. He argued that it is the Reagan administration which has been willing to intensify the military approach since 1981, with a view to destroying the opposition rather than negotiating. It is the Reagan administration not the opposition which is trying to gain time. The FDR talks with the American special envoy Richard Stone and with the Salvadoran Peace Commission are frozen because of the US and the Salvadoran government. These talks with Stone and the Peace Commission are essentially cosmetic, to appease American and international public opinion. Ungo illustrated this by his claim that President Magana and the Salvadoran Peace Commission say they are for talks, yet do not accept that they should be held in San Salvador (either in an Embassy or the nuncio's residence). As he put it 'how can we **participate in an electoral campaign if there is no chance of our delegation even talking in San Salvador?'**

In summary, Ungo claimed that the opposition has been consistently in favour of negotations. The agenda should deal with (1) the army, (2) the elections, (3) a broadly-based new government, (4) reforms and (5) non-alignment. He stressed that the main aim of a negotiated settlement would be to put an end to the war; that the opposition forces would not aim to play a dominant role in a provisional government, but also that it does not accept that the Right for its part should dominate the provisional government. He stressed that El Salvador was going to need private enterprise, and that **the opposition's programme 'is anti-oligarchic, not anti-capitalist'.** He also claimed that it was only through such a provisional government, with a programme both for democratic elections and a democratic regime that both peace and progress could be brought to the country.

PART FOUR - HONDURAS

Some circles in the United States claim that Honduras is a bastion of freedom and model of democracy in an otherwise troubled region. Regrettably, the model is flawed on closer inspection.

Chronic Poverty

It is internationally recognised that Honduras is not only one of the poorest countries in the region, but one of the poorest in the world. The statistics should shock, yet only scratch the surface of the problem. Some million and a quarter people exist in a state of total poverty. Some quarter of a million people are registered as unemployed and the average family size is five persons in a country with no social security or basic welfare provision.

The distribution of land is unjust in the extreme. Just over 1.1% of the agricultural population own some 40% of the land. Most of the best land is owned by the banana companies. Nearly a third of land is not properly cultivated.

Yet, when discussing the priority given by the United States to land reform in El Salvador with Mr Shepard Lowman of the United States Embassy in Tegucigalpa, we asked him what was the parallel pressure for such reform. He replied that 'there is no need for land reform in Honduras'.

We find this astonishing in view of the fact that, according to Julian Mendez, President of ANACH (Asociacion Nacional de Campesinos de Honduras), some 140,000 people still have no land of their own in an economy where sixty per cent of work opportunities are in agriculture, where subsistence farming is the base of survival and where there are no essential welfare services such as obtain, for instance, in Costa Rica.

In this context, when so much is heard in US circles about their pressure for land reform in El Salvador, and so little in Honduras it is hard to avoid the conclusion that the United States' concern in the region is not for land reform in its own right but as a factor in counter-insurgency strategy in individual countries.

According to the Collegio de Medicos (the Honduran medical association) basic health care provision does not reach 60% of the population in the countryside. It is officially recognised that there is massive under-employment outside the main urban areas, in the campo – with even the claim of a figure of ninety per cent, plus up to sixty per cent of those in registered employment in fact under-employed. Average income in industry is over US $4 a day, but only an estimated $1.27 in the agricultural sector. Two thirds of Honduran families do not receive enough to satisfy basic nutritional needs, and over 70% of Honduran children under the age of five are malnourished. One fifth of the population in Honduras commands 70% of the income, with the remaining four fifths gaining what they can of the rest.

Economic Dependence

The Honduran economy is totally dependent on the world market. From the end of the nineteenth century, US mining and banana companies reduced the country to an enclave economy. It is notable that Tegucigalpa is among a handful of capitals in the world without a railway station, due to the fact that the United Fruit Company built its railway lines straight from the banana plantations to the ports.

After the Second World War Honduras began to follow a strategy of import-substituting industrialisation. But this only gained real momentum in the 1960's. Moreover, according to government evidence to the Kissinger Commission 'while national industry has grown significantly by eight per cent this has not been enough to generate surplus for export which has made the sector a strong drain on foreign exchange;

neither has it significantly increased employment.'

External dependence has made the Honduran economy vulnerable both to variations in world market prices, and the decisions of foreign capital. Recurrent food crises occur as a result of a fall in the production of basic grains. At the same time small scale industry has been marginalised by the industrial programme, with the emergence of a dual domestic economy. Small firms either have been excluded or have not proportionately gained from government technical and financial aid. At the same time, **the profits made in the viable part of the Honduran private sector have tended to accumulate in foreign banks** rather than reinvestment in Honduras. The so-called indigenous Honduran private sector failed to take advantage of the captive internal market it gained when Honduras withdrew from the Central American Common Market after the 1969 war with El Salvador.

Loan contracting and aid disbursement by the government in the 1970's has tended to be self-defeating. For instance, in the period 1976-78 it followed a strategy of contracting large foreign loans, which it then distributed to the private sector via the government body CONADI (National Council for Industrial Development). Corruption, theft and the tactic of declaring bankrupt the firm which contracted the loan left CONADI with large debts.

Economic Crisis

The result is an acute economic crisis. Honduras now has a balance of payments deficit of $220 million, a fiscal deficit of over $300 million and a foreign debt of some $1650 million. Its major source of internally generated foreign exchange - agro-export - has fallen in value by 30% between 1980 and 1983, whilst foreign capital coming into the country fell by over 50% between 1980 and 1982. This has had devastating implications for an economy which has to import the majority of its material inputs and goods and services — and which has traditionally relied on foreign loans to provide the majority of investment capital.

Interest on Honduras' foreign debt, plus payments on foreign investment, represented over 50% of the balance of payments deficit in 1981, and an estimated 75% of the deficit for 1982. Honduras is presently negotiating the rescheduling of $120 million of its debt with private banks. At the same time it is seeking the continued support of the IMF, which is demanding further stringent austerity measures.

It is clear that aid resulting from the recommendations of the Kissinger Commission may meet some of Honduras' financial needs in the short term. However, granted the problems of profoundly unequal distribution of land, wealth and income, the large number of landless people, the dualism of the traditional and modern sectors of the economy plus continued external dependence on export outlets dominated by a few foreign companies — **we cannot see how aid without accompanying fundamental reforms in the social and economic structure of the country can resolve its basic economic problems.**

Disappearing Aid

This is besides the evident corruption in aid disbursement and apart from the literal disappearance of aid recently given by international agencies.

The most dramatic example involves the Minister of Education in the appropriation of milk donated by the EEC.

In July 1983, the ex-supervisor of food for schoolchildren (alimentation escolar), Miriam Zaval de Avila, denounced the disappearance of 200 tons of non-vitaminised powdered milk, valued at approximately $200,000, which had been a donation from the EEC to the Ministry of Education.

Well documented evidence was produced which showed that while the bags were loaded into lorries they never arrived at their intended destination. A number of them reappeared in the markets of Tegucigalpa and San Pedro Sula.

Two months later, in September, the amount of disappeared milk had risen to 400 tons, worth approximately $400,000.

The official response to the demands of Eberhardt Goll, then Coordinator of the EEC programme in Honduras, who demanded a complete explanation from the government, was to accuse him of having sympathies with the Sandinista government in Nicaragua, and eventually to declare him **persona non grata**. Goll had no option but to leave Honduras.

The 'milk affair' continues unresolved: EEC aid to the value of approximately $32 million continues to the country.

The Government's Response

The government's response so far to the economic crisis has been:

- to cut public spending, with drastic cuts in the budgets of the Ministries of Health, Education, Natural Resources (Agrarian Reform), Transport and Works;

- to encourage more foreign investment via two new laws: the Bilateral Investment Treaty with the US and the Law for Export Promotion which give wide guarantees to the private sector and foreign enterprise;

- to encourage foreign investment via negotiations with the OPI (Overseas Private Investment Corporation) and the Council of Commerce in New Orleans, particularly export-oriented light industry;

- to pass a Law of Economic Emergency (on which more later);

- to 'streamline' the financial banking system;

- to freeze incomes in an already unusually low wage economy;

- to devalue the currency, with the risk of high inflationary pressure.

In our view these measures are unlikely to resolve the basic problems in the economy, even if they stave off bankruptcy in the short term.

Foreign investors are unlikely to risk investment in Honduras, while the region remains in turmoil and Honduras potentially at war.

For similar reasons, plus Honduras' difficulties in paying its foreign debt, foreign banks are unlikely to give the massive aid required by Honduras.

The increasing regional and local tensions are unlikely to provide an 'ideal investment climate'.

The strategy resolves none of the structural problems of the Honduran economy. Rather, by increasing foreign indebtedness, whilst following the previous policy of concentration in agro-export industries and 'finishing' industries, it intensifies them.

Democracy in Question

Honduras is put forward by the Reagan administration as the 'democratic alternative' for Central America, while the Honduran government and Armed Forces present themselves before international and national opinion as the 'defenders of peace and democracy in the region'. Certainly transition to a genuinely functioning democracy, after fifteen years of military rule is be fraught with difficulties. There is no doubt that the majority of Hondurans want to live in a democracy based on the western model: the massive turnout (over eighty per cent) in the 1981 elections, and the overwhelming majority (over fifty per cent) gained by the Liberal Party - until recently seen as the anti-military party - is evidence to that effect.

However, **the legitimacy of the dominant Liberal Party is open to question.**

In August 1983 it held internal elections. These were widely recognised to be a fraud aimed at maintaining the control of the dominant Rodista faction against the social democratic tendency of ALIPO (Alianza Liberal del Pueblo). For example, the Rodista faction gained more votes in its favour in just Tegucigalpa, than the entire number of votes cast in the whole of the department of Francisco Morazon (of which Tegucigalpa is a part) in the General Elections of 1981.

Also, **there are clear questions whether the present position of Honduras could be defined as a democracy,** and they appear to be growing as the internal situation polarises and US foreign policy strengthens the power of the Honduran military. This has lead increasing sectors of the Honduran political centre to define the present government as a 'civilian-military' regime; other commentators, further to the left, have defined it as a National Security State. Significantly, the Reverend Sun Myung Moon, head of the Unification Church, was welcomed and given every facility to preach his anti-Communist message or crusade, while a group of US 'nuns for peace' were summarily expelled from the country.

Congress Undermined

For instance, the Ley de Emergencia Economica - the Economic Emergency Law passed in one day, 25 November 1983, despite an outcry from the opposition gives the Executive the **Power to take all the financial and economic measures necessary to reactivate the national economy, without reference to Congress.** The argument for it was that going through Congress would take too long in view of the urgency of the situation. **Congress now controls neither the armed forces nor the economy.** Thus the way has now been paved for the real running of the country by a civilian-military cabal consisting of APROH (Associacion para el Progresso de Honduras), the Armed Forces and the Executive.

Manipulation of the Judiciary

The judicial system in Honduras is widely known to be corrupt and subject to political pressure and favouritism. This has caused two scandals recently. On November 22 the judge of Santa Rosade Copan resigned, citing pressure from the President of the Supreme Court and the Liberal Party for him to sack one of his judges and replace him with a favoured member of the Liberal Party. The following week the Chief Criminal Judge in San Pedro Sula was sacked for issuing a warrant for the arrest of the Head of the Pentitentiary in San Pedro Sula on the basis of evidence that he had received a bribe of $7500 to facilitate the escape of a prisoner. This man happened to be the godfather of an adviser to the Government, while his son is married to the daughter of the President of the Executive Committee of the Liberal Party.

The Armed Forces

The armed forces play a key political role in the country. Not only do they constantly pronounce on policy - hardly a day passes without one of them making an aggressive reference to Nicaragua - but their structural relationship with the government is closer and more effective than between it and Congress.

In Honduras the armed forces also control the police, FUSEP (Fuerzas de Seguridad de Policia); the security services of the DNI (Departamento Nacional e Investigaciones); G2 (military intelligence) and the Comites del Defensa Civil (Civil Defence Committees).

Before he came to power, President Roberto Suazo Cordova, then presidential candidate, made an agreement with General Gustavo Alvarez Martinez, that a Liberal government would not investigate charges of corruption against the outgoing military regime. It has not.

The Armed Forces retain complete autonomy

over all matters concerning military and security affairs inside the country - national security, policy, budget and spending, training, internal structure and promotions, priorities and activities. President Suazo Cordova is nominally Commander-in-Chief of the Armed Forces, but there is no question that the power lies with General Alvarez.

There is a close relationship between the Armed Forces view of the world and economic policy. General Gustavo Alvarez is the President of APROH, which groups together military, leading private sector members and professionals into a right wing think-tank. From recent confidential memoranda published in El Tiempo it is clear that APROH was responsible for drafting Suazo Cordova's letters to President Reagan requesting $350-400 million in urgent aid. **APROH has played, and is playing a central role in influencing government foreign and economic policy.** In one of its confidential memos published in El Tiempo it called for the US to intervene directly in Nicaragua. APROH's links with the military were highlighted in the memorandum published in El Tiempo of 9 December 1983, where APROH proposes:

> 'the idea of organising a 'social-forestry system' which would incorporate 125,000 campesino families, organised into cooperatives and beneath obligatory military service, in order to assure care of forestry, create new sources of employment and income, and strengthen internal security against subversion.'
> i.e. create paramilitary groups under the control of the Armed Forces.

Further, in the midst of stringent budget cuts - particularly affecting welfare services - the defence and national security budget remains the same.

Theoretically, the actions of the Armed Forces are constrained by certain provisions of the Constitution and the Law. In practice, both have been openly violated. According to the

Constitution all movements of foreign troops in national territory and all military agreements with other countries should be previously agreed by Congress. The agreement for the installation of the CREM (Centro Regional de Entrenamiento Militar) in Puerto Castilla was secretly negotiated by General Alvarez and the Pentagon before it became known to Congress or the public.

Human Rights

Violations of human rights have increased since the civilian government took office. In 1982 there were 25 disappearances, 386 politically motivated arrests, and 95 murders involving the security forces. Forty bodies were found in clandestine graves. Despite Honduras' Habeus Corpus laws, people continue to disappear and to be held without trial. In June, Mayor Juan Blas Salazar, Head of the DNI security force admitted to having disappeared people in the DNI cells, but justified his disregard of the law on the grounds that national security overrode considerations of Habeus Corpus (La Tribuna, 10 June 1983). He has not been charged and continues as head of DNI. While the numbers of people disappeared, tortured and/or killed are relatively small compared to El Salvador and Guatemala, the increasing power of the security apparatus gives cause for serious concern.

The courts have declined to intervene, despite repeated appeals from COFADEH (Comite of the Families of the Detained and Disappeared of Honduras), while investigation has been left to the accused perpetrators of the offences — the DNI.

In 1983 there have been 15 political murders. Moreover, the DNI brought before the courts 49 people who had been kidnapped, tortured in clandestine jails, and held incommunicado for long periods

Intimidation

Intimidation is widespread in Honduras. For instance, Comites de Defensa are local village or barrio 'neighbourhood' committees whose job it is to watch for suspicious activities and who are obliged to make monthly reports to the armed forces. These Committees are certainly functioning in the countryside and according to independent eye-witnesses, have created a climate of fear and intimidation. Again this is cause for concern, not least because 'denounced' people do not have recourse to law to prove their innocence. They represent a clear trend in Honduras towards intimidation and repression of local populations by both the security and armed forces.

Such intimidation also is illustrated by the extent to which the Honduran government and the armed forces have systematically tried to neutralise the popular movement, to ensure that there is not internal opposition to either US foreign policy or to the practice of 'democracy'. This has taken a number of forms:

i) the assasination of key trade union leaders, such as Herminio Dera and five other leaders on the North coast;

ii) the arrest of key trade union and campesino leaders, such as Francisco Menjivar Suarez of the Water Workers Trade Union and Victor Inocencio Peralta of the National Farmworkers Union;

iii) the creation of government-backed 'Frente Democraticos' - Democratic Fronts - who, on a technicality challenge the elected Left leadership, and the are recognised as the official leadership by the government and the Supreme Court.

Limits to Opposition

Opposition does exist in Honduras, but its open expression has been largely confined to isolated protests by individuals such as Efrain Diaz Arriviallaga, the lone Christian Democrat Congressman, Ramon Custodio, and recently by the Teachers' Union. Open opposition from the trade unions and peasants organisations has been limited to the level of paid advertisements in the press.

The lack of organised opposition is due (1) partly to the faith invested in the government to bring about peaceful change after the elections; (2) to intimidation by the army and security apparatus; (3) the absence of strong parliamentary opposition and (4) partly to the internal divisions in the popular movement.

In our view, such current weakness does not diminish the force of the principle claims on which the opposition groups are agreed including:

i) economic and fiscal reforms to ease the burden of the bulk of the population;

ii) an end to human rights violations and the repression of unions and other popular organisation;

iii) a change in foreign policy, including the adoption of a Costa Rican style neutrality and a refusal to become involved in armed conflict, either in Nicaragua or El Salvador;

iv) an end to political sectarianism by the government determining civil service appointments;

v) restoration of civilian control over government and guarantees of clean elections in 1984 (municipal) and 1985 (presidential).

Summary

In short, there is a progressive weakening of the civil power and the institutionalisation of a security apparatus, as Honduras is turned into a counter-revolutionary base or US garrison state. The radical Right feel secure under US protection and have abandoned interest in reform which now appears unnecessary to preserve the peace; the emphasis is on the destruction of the revolution in Nicaragua, by for example reforming the CONDECA alliance rather than on desperately needed social and agrarian reform. The increasing social polarisation and reduction in civilian autonomy is largely due to the distortion of domestic priorities caused by the US military presence and pressure. It is said that there are negotiations over the permanent stationing of US military personnel in the country as a follow-up to the succession of Big Pine exercises. Changes will come, but the effect of US policy has been to make it more likely that such changes will be violent rather than peaceful.

PART FIVE - NICARAGUA

During our visit we met the non-resident British Ambassador, the Chamorro brothers, editors respectively of the opposition daily La Prensa and of the Sandinista daily Barricada, the Deputy Minister of Foreign Affairs, the Ambassadors to the Contadora countries, Comandante Carlos Nunez Tellez, The President of the National Assembly, Dr Sergio Ramirez of the governing junta. We also met Deputy Director of the FIR (National Reconstruction Fund) and other economists including Xavier Gorostiaga of the Institute of Economic and Social Research (INIES), which has played a key role in the Hague Declaration on an alternative economic strategy for Central America.

We took evidence from trades unionists and also the several parties constituting the Patriotic Front of the revolution. We regret to say that because of a refusal on the part of the church hierarchy, we did not meet with Catholic leaders. Also, due to a misunderstanding we did not meet with the opposition Coordinadora Democratica on the first day of our visit. We proposed to them an alternative meeting on the third day of our visit, but apparently they felt that they could not arrange this.

The most incongruous part of our visit was the leisured drink and discussion with the United States Ambassador Anthony C. Quainton - diplomatic representative to a country which his government is doing its utmost to destabilise by military, economic, political and diplomatic means. The CIA not only are arming and supporting the Contras both in Honduras and in Costa Rica - the Reagan administration also has slashed the sugar quota and effectively vetoed the provision of special funds from the Inter-American Development Bank, inter alia for much-needed social projects. It is clearly plausible that the United States is directly encouraging internal destabilisation of both the Sandinista government and the revolution through some opposition groups in the country. Although we had no direct evidence to support this, diplomatically, the United States stalling on the Stone talks and its unwillingness to back the Contadora initiative is public knowledge.

Indeed, progress in this and other fields depends on the USA. Over the past few months there has emerged a package of changes in Nicaraguan policies - in the direction of national reconciliation and pluralism - amnesty to Contras and Miskito indians, withdrawal of some Cuban advisors etc. **With some justification the Sandinistas ask at what point they can expect an appropriate US response.**

We have no doubt that the Sandinistas enjoy majority popular support - overwhelming among the young in a country where half the population is under 16. Much of the old middle class is more or less alienated as a result of the loss of its previous economic privilege. The article by Arturo J. Cruz, a former member of the Junta, in the Summer 1983 issue of Foreign Affairs illustrates disaffected political opinion.

But there is an expectancy of a US invasion shared even by opposition Pedro Chamorro of La Prensa. Arms have been widely distributed to the Nicaraguan people. But no government which feared for its popular support - and certainly no dictatorship - would arm its people. Professionals and workers showed us the air raid shelters they had dug against possible US or Salvadoran air attack. Constant incursions by the Contras have failed to establish a 'liberated' area as a basis for international recognition.

Clearly mistakes have been made - censorship in part justified on grounds of national security but often apparently capricious, an unsympathetic attempt to impose standardised policies on the Miskito indians long politically isolated and culturally different, a hamfisted treatment of the Pope's visit and a number of clumsy relations with senior churchmen.

But much of the explanation is due to inexperience, over-enthusiasm and attempts at de-stabilisation from abroad. **It is clear to us** that by their economic and military siege the Reagan administration is creating a justification for the very internal and foreign policies they purport to criticise.

Democracy

The Reagan caricature of a Marxist totalitarian state run by sinister Cubans and apparatchiks is absurd. For instance, contrary to widespread claims that Nicaragua constantly toes the Soviet line in Security Council voting, on a crucial vote such as Afghanistan the Nicaraguans in fact abstained rather than voted with the Soviets, and also have differed from them on a number of other occasions.

There is a range of opinion within the Sandinista FSLN itself, a healthy private sector and a spread of bilateral aid (22 per cent from socialist countries, 32 per cent from Latin America, 5 per cent from Africa, Asia and the rest mostly from Western Europe).

It should be impossible for those open to evidence to claim that Nicaragua is a monolithic one-party state heading inevitably for a Cuban or Eastern European model. In reality despite declarations on Marxist-Leninism by leading individuals, **the Nicaraguan revolution embodies three powerful ideologies - Christ, the liberator of the poor, Marx, the 'liberator' of the people, and Sandino, the national patriot.** Whether any of these forces ultimately will dominate Nicaraguan society will depend in substantial part on the policy of the United States.

Elections

The elections promised at the time of the revolution have not yet taken place. Certainly, the explanations given by the Sandinistas themselves are open to question, and we recognise that they remain vulnerable on this point. However, we have already stressed that US pressure for instant elections in Nicaragua has not been matched over many years by similar pressure for elections in dictatorships throughout Central and Latin America. Second, it certainly is clear that if the Nicaraguans had called elections immediately following the success of the revolution that they could have then established what amounted to a one-party state. Third, there are genuine issues concerning both the mode of election and the form of government in a country unaccustomed to changing government by ballot rather than bullet. Fourth, the country is on a war footing because of the incursions by the Contras and the threat of invasion by the United States.

Few Western democracies have proceeded with general elections during hostilities with other countries. In Britain, even during the period of 'phoney war' with Nazi Germany, the main parties entered into a coalition paralleling a government of National Unity and suspended both general elections and contests in by-elections.

In the event, Comandante Nunez took the opportunity of our meeting with him to publish for the first time a specific schedule and timetable for the preparation of elections in 1985, beginning from January this year.

We are persuaded that the election schedule is genuine and confident that the government intends to ensure that they are a democratic test of public opinion. We emphasise that this is more than our finding on the elections proposed in El Salvador in March this year. Not least, we are struck by the lack of internal terror or repression in Nicaragua, and the total lack of any claim of the use of torture. In contrast with El Salvador, this gives an effective rather than purely formal freedom of choice to the Nicaraguan people to express their own will for their own future form of government.

Pluralism

It is clear that while there were only **two** parties in Somoza's Nicaragua (his Liberals and the Conservatives) there now are **eleven** parties operating in the country, quite apart from independent centres of opinion and publicity such as the church. It was the representatives of the Popular Social Christian Party, the Socialist Party and the Liberal Party – separate from the Sandinistas though cooperating with the FSLN – who made to us the point that the Sandinistas could have held elections in 1980, but then would have been called opportunistic, and that the case for delay was to normalise conditions and prepare real elections of a kind that Nicaragua had never had before. The representatives of these parties stressed that despite the external military and economic pressures, they were convinced that elections would occur and would be for real.

It also was these non-Sandinist party representatives who stressed to us the extent to which the remaining opposition parties represented the former oligarchy and its interests, which in their view substantially explained their disaffection from the regime. As they put it, the parties of the Right are those which have been displaced from socio-economic power. They added that some of them certainly sought to destabilise both the Sandinistas and the revolution in Nicaragua and that in their view 'they must accept the new framework, and not destabilise it.'

A leading representative of the Liberal Party stressed to us 'I am a Liberal not a Marxist' but who also said that he supported the revolution and was entirely opposed to outside intervention. As he put it, in 1909 a Liberal government was returned which tried to challenge the power of vested interests in the big estates of the Latifundia, but three years later the marines came in. He also bluntly criticised the view of the Reagan administration and it was he – not Sandinistas – who put to us that 'Nicaragua is not an East-West problem – it is a North-South problem'.

Other representatives of the non-Sandinist parties whom we saw admitted that the exercise of power in Nicaragua is not neutral, but questioned whether it was so by the Reagan administration in the United States, and underlined that the current exercise of power is 'directed to the welfare of the majority'. Questioned by us on the limits to amnesty for former Somocistas or Contras in the run-up to the elections, the same independent party representatives asked in return whether we had considered the parallel of Great Britain and Northern Ireland, where neither **Labour nor Conservative governments have welcomed terrorists to the conference table.**

Clearly there are those among the leadership of the Sandinists who have stressed the concept of a vanguard party. However, in the case of Nicaragua there is no question that the Sandinistas were the vanguard of the popular revolution which overthrew Somoza – they were literally at the front when others now in opposition or exile were politically deprived but economically privileged under the Somoza regime. In this sense, the vanguard role of the Sandinistas has been national and reflects widespread popular support. **To consider the Sandinistas in the same terms as the Bolsheviks is politically illiterate. It is as absurd as considering that the Mitterrand government in France is Marxist-Leninist because it includes some Ministers from the French Communist Party.**

Trades Unions

We met and took evidence at length from trades unionists in Nicaragua, which further confirmed our view that in this as in other sectors an effective pluralism flourishes in the country.

Before July 1979 less then 7 per cent of the working population was trade unionised and the bargaining power of trades unions further reduced inasmuch as the five main union federations represented just over one per cent of the economically active population.

By contrast, there now are literally hundreds of trade unions in Nicaragua. This reflects the continuation of pre-revolutionary structures and organisation into the post-revolutionary period, in other words trades unions in Nicaragua were based on factories and companies rather than trades or industries. No effort was made by the Sandinistas after the revolution to force trades unions into vertical monolithic structures rather than continue with a workplace branch organisation.

The CAUS Communist Party Union and the Frente Obrera, which amounts to a Maoist union, both are minoritised through lack of popular support, and there is an emerging plural and federal structure of unions including ANDEN or the Teachers' Association; ATC (for rural workers); UPN (for journalists); FETSALUD (for health workers) etc.

While the Sandinista CST central union federation is the biggest and represents more than 500 branches, the CGTI of the Socialist Party of Nicaragua asserts an influential role. Also, there clearly is a pluralist cooperative framework in the CSN, or National Union Committee equivalent in form to the Trades Union Congress in Great Britain, which includes the majority of currents, trends and tendencies inside the trade union movement.

The right-wing CUS trade union committee linked with the Conservative Party and the Constitutional Liberals (a remnant of Somoza's former party) now have some 3,000 affiliate members, but is clearly in a small minority in relation to the CST with over 110,000 affiliate members.

When we asked whether the CSN/CST were able to pursue independent free collective bargaining, their representatives told us that in the immediate post-revolutionary period they had pursued independent claims but – despite the right of trades unions to strike – they found it hard to consider industrial action in view of the fact that virtually from the first days of the Reagan administration credits to Nicaragua had been suspended at a time when the struggle for independence against the Somoza regime had virtually bankrupted the country.

The right to strike clearly exists in Nicaragua. The bodies representing the overwhelming majority of trades unionists refused to implement it precisely because of the internal and external difficulties faced by the country, not least due to pressure from the Reagan administration.

Press Censorship

We have already commented in some detail on the practice of press censorship in Nicaragua, stressing the parallel with UK and US government press restrictions during the Falklands and Grenada invasions.

When we saw Pedro Chamorro, he told us that he 'does not believe that the government wants to shut down La Prensa', which has a daily circulation of between 50,000 and 60,000. Pedro Chamorro also said that in his view the state-owned media should be state and not party, and that the Contras should not be called such rather than 'armed opponents of the regime'.

We see the point of his observation on separating state and party press, although in Western terms any state press (rather than official news bulletins) tends to be unacceptable, while a Party press is common in many countries (apart from the freedom of press owners to give specific support to Parties including the government parties).

He also confirmed (1) that he sends photocopied material of censored material to embassies in Managua, and although he claims protests were made to him about this, the government did not stop this practice; (2) that he is free to post copies of censored material on the extensive metal railings outside the offices of La Prensa, where they can be read by members of the public.

While the posting of censored material to be viewed from the street — even in the capital — clearly falls short of press freedom — it also is evident that the circulation of censored material to embassies in Managua gives an international outlet for the paper which is very considerable.

We were especially interested in comments on the same issues by Pedro's brother, Carlos,

editor of Barricada, who stressed that his paper
- the official organ of the Sandinista Front for
National Liberation - also was censored in the
same way on a daily basis. But he added that
this was overwhelmingly on military material,
understandable in a sizable country where
confirmation of claims, for instance on
incursion of Contras, were genuinely difficult
to confirm. Normally such material was cleared
by the government after a delay of two or three
hours. Stressing that is his view such
censorship was necessary, and making the analogy
with the Falklands and Grenada, Carlos Chamorro
also asked us how the United Kingdom or US
government would respond to invasion of their
country by several hundred thousand or a million
Contras, when on a proportional basis this would
be the position.

He also claimed to us that La Prensa is not
the same paper as won worldwide international
respect before the assassination of their
father. He worked there in 1978-79, and in 1980
a split occurred on the editorial policy being
pursued against the fundamental aims of the
revolution. He put to us that 85% of the former
editorial staff and correspondents left La
Prensa in March-April 1980, including both
himself and his uncle, who now edits El Nuevo
Diario.

Further, on the claim of press freedom,
Carlos Chamorro pointed out that the Church has
both a radio and weekly paper (El Tayacan) with
a circulation of up to 10,000. He said that
Nuevo Diario has a circulation of some 40,000,
Barricada up to 90,000, and La Prensa around
50,000.

Miskitos and Others

It was made plain to us both before and
during our visit that we could if we wished
visit the Atlantic/Caribbean seaboard and the
Miskito areas. However, due to the difficulties
of travel, even by air, this could have limited
some of the rest of our agenda in Nicaragua. We
spent the day instead driving to the Esteli

region and to the border post at El Espino. However, we took independent evidence on the Miskito problem from non-government sources including Britons involved with the aid and cooperation programme in the region.

From these independent sources it was put to us that certainly mistakes had been made in handling the Miskito problem - as indeed now is openly admitted by the government. The main fault lay in seeking to impose on a culturally and linguistically different region an organisation found to be well suited to the Western seaboard areas.

On the other hand, it also was put to us that the physical isolation of the Eastern seaboard of Nicaragua is underestimated in some of the foreign press and media comment. Somoza never completed a road link through to the area, and most of the Zelaya region on the Eastern seaboard (mainly jungle, and covering much of the land mass of the country) had been neglected or left to foreign interests until the Sandinista revolution. Neither the Miskito indians (estimated variously as from 80 to 120,000) nor the Sumu (some 5 to 6,000) nor the 50,000 creoles in the area had been acclimatised to Spanish culture or institutions. The main cultural influence to the mid-19th century was British, and thereafter North American through US mining companies.

The culture gap following the revolution can be illustrated by the fact that in the early stages of the literacy campaign there was not even a basic dictionary of the Miskito language.

The efforts made to provide land reform, housing, health programmes, schools and infrastructure in the 'free lands' meant that **the Sandinistas were were doing more for the Indians than the Spanish peasants or campesinos** in the surrounding areas who - being more dispersed - gained less directly from the facilities concerned.

Political mistakes were made in seeking to overcome the lack of local organisation on the Atlantic coast by undue reliance on Stedman Fagoth, a former Somocista agent whose activities helped disorient the Misurasata organisation (Sandinistas, Miskitos and Sumu) and who (following first prison and then later house arrest) rejoined the Somocistas.

The whole campaign to provide a modern social and economic infrastructure in the region is being regularly attacked by the Contras. As a result of sniper attacks doctors sponsored by the Catholic Institute for International Relations who were supposed to undertake primary health care in rural areas have had to be withdrawn to Bluefields. Development on a water project financed by Oxfam and the British Overseas Development Administration at Tasbapri has been stopped following a sniper attack on one of the engineers.

Such attacks show the double standards of the United States administration in claiming that it is concerned to bring economic aid and development to the region while financing, backing and legitimating the activities of the Contras in Nicaragua. **Clearly, the forceful removal of Miskitos from the areas bordering Honduras was deeply resented,** and provoked some of them to cross the border and join the Contras. **But their withdrawal could have been less necessary if the United States had not helped translate the frontier into a war zone.**

Nonetheless, eye-witness sources put to us that, despite the initial problems, the Miskitos were now beginning to realise the benefits of the $15 million dollars expenditure on land reform, housing, health, education, water supply and electrification programmes.

The Literacy Campaign

We were sceptical before our arrival about the claims for advances in the literacy among the peasant population following the national literacy crusade of 1980. The Nicaraguan authorities themselves claim that the adult literacy campaign has only begun. The British volunteers we met, reflecting their experience in the field, confirmed to us that there had in fact been a major reduction in illiteracy, and that the continuing adult literacy campaign was a success. We were impressed by the key role played by Oxfam in this area.

We appreciate that this in itself does not meet the claim made by some that the literacy campaign is indoctrination and propaganda. Certainly it is clear that, when taught to read, previously illiterate people also are shown by example and in language what their teachers — overwhelmingly supporting the revolution — consider to be the major social and economic advances achieved since the overthrow of Somoza.

In our view it seems likely that if there is any problem in this respect it is one of over-enthusiasm rather than an organised propaganda campaign. There also are real gains for formerly illiterate peasants where ability to read and understand relates to the direct improvement of their economic condition. For example, an American theatre group described the pleasure on the faces of campesinos able to read and understand the titles to the land which they had received.

The flourishing of the literacy campaign in Nicaragua is outstanding in relation to the appalling illiteracy and the lack of virtually any campaign to counter it in neighbouring Honduras.

The Health Campaign

We took the opportunity to visit a health centre in Esteli on our return from the Northern frontier region. This was a spontaneous visit, arranged at a few minutes notice. The health centre was a small converted motel, with its number of small bedrooms converted into consulting rooms.

The formal structure of the health centre compared with a local group practice in the British National Health Service (three general doctors, two paediatricians, two gynaecologists and one psychiatrist with three graduate nurses). But there were crucial differences. For one thing, unlike a local group practice in the United Kingdom, the health centre was responsible for 80,000 inhabitants and 120 communities in a region as big as an English county or a French department. Second, unlike most group practices in Britain, the health centre also provided dental treatment. Third, there was a marked lack of modern basic equipment (with the exception of a dental x-ray machine). Fourth, there was an evident lack of basic medicines, surgical equipment, and laboratory chemicals and equipment. Fifth, it was reported that the centre treated some 600 to 700 people a day, 6 days a week, sometimes with three doctors per consultancy room.

The centre lacked the facilities, staff and equipment to do surgical work. It referred the most serious cases to the hospital in Esteli, but this has only 120 beds to cater for the population of 80,000 in the region, while the main surgical hospital for the region was in the town of La Trinidad.

We were impressed by such a model of health centre care. However, it was clear that the centre in Esteli was under-funded, under-equipped, under-supplied and overworked. Granted that the emphasis was on preventative medical care and in going out to reach those in the campo who previously had gained neither medical nor dental treatment, we are not surprised that the staff of the centre whom we met, and the representatives of staff associations, welcomed the assistance of 12 Cuban doctors in the region who had not left by December 1983. It appeared that those Cubans who had left had been teachers. In response to our question, and according to a local woman who was receiving treatment at the centre during our visit 'it is a load of ordure to claim that the Cubans are military advisers.'

A British volunteer doctor on the Atlantic coast was quick to praise the competence and dedication of his Cuban colleagues and the tremendous blow to the local health services which would result if they were forced to leave.

We were not able to go into the campo to check the authenticity of the claims concerning an outwards preventative care strategy, but this has already been documented elsewhere by others in considerable detail. We are persuaded that **the emphasis placed on paediatrics, gynaecology, dental care and vaccination is real and effective** for working people and peasants who in some of the neighbouring countries have no access to health facilities. In this context we recall the claim made by the Collegio de Medicos in Honduras that medical care does not reach 60% of the population. By contrast, it was claimed to us in the health centre at Esteli that such care does reach 85% of the population of the region, and that the lapse on the rest frequently occurs because women in particular, having been vaccinated or checked for the first time, do not necessarily return to the health posts for which the health centre is responsible. Attempts to 'follow up' are limited in some cases by lack of personnel and adequate resources, including insufficient transport.

The Economy

It is clear that the Nicaraguan government is directing economic resources, without corruption and without privilege, towards basic social needs. This was evident not only in the health sector but also in the re-housing programme, including rehousing from areas threatened by flooding in Managua itself, which we visited.

The costs of the civil war were devastating in a country lacking democratic means to overthrow Somoza. It has been estimated by the time the war ended that unemployment had risen to 30%, that inflation was touching 60% and that real domestic product had fallen back nearly 20 years to the level of 1962.

Against this legacy, and by third world standards, the economic record of the Sandinistas has been most impressive. The reconstruction growth rate in 1980 was over 10%, and in 1981 7%. The economy faltered badly in 1982, with a negative growth rate, although this was almost exactly paralleled by the rest of the Central American region in that year due in part to drought and flood.

Since the revolution the FSLN appears to have halved unemployment (the latest figures put the number of jobless at 14%, despite an upward trend).

Also, according to the Review of the Bank of London and South America of February 1983 'the (Sandinista) government has continued to honour all foreign debt commitments of the previous regime'. As the Washington Post put it in July last year: 'despite the US charge that the economy is weak, Nicaragua until last month was one of the few countries in Latin America to avoid falling behind in repaying loans from foreign commercial banks'.

The Cuts in Aid

Apart from such readiness to meet debt obligations, the 'basic needs' approach to development has doubled the share of GDP spent in Nicaragua on education within three years. Health campaigns have produced an abrupt fall in infant mortality virtually abolishing tetanus and massively reducing the incidence of malaria. Against this background it is little short of scandalous that the Reagan administration appears to pride itself on the rigour with which it has cut economic aid to Nicaragua.

Multinational funding for Nicaragua has virtually dried up. Nicaraguan officials speak of a boycott and present these interesting figures of multilateral financial assistance to their country since the FSLN took over.

	1979	1980	1981	1982	1983
World Bank	-	57.0	49.7	-	-
Inter-American Development Bank	113.5	67.6	8.0	34.4	1.0

Heavily dependent upon a few commodities and suffering as much as any country from the recession, Nicaragua faces foreign exchange shortages. By contrast, between 1980 and 1983, multinational institutions have channelled

$1,965 million into El Salvador, Honduras, Guatemala and Costa Rica.

There is no doubt that under US pressure, bodies like the World Bank are holding back funds which a country like Nicaragua would normally expect. Three major World Bank loans, relating to infrastructural projects, are currently frozen. Bank officials maintain that the ratio of Nicaragua's debt service payments to foreign exchange earnings presents too high an investment risk.

The World Bank position is absurd and discriminatory considering the very high level of multinational investment which finds its way into Mexico, only recently on the verge of a full scale default.

Reagan administration spokesmen have said in public that the USA will oppose multilateral loans to Nicaragua on political grounds. In June 1983, the USA vetoed a proposal put before the Inter-American Development Bank to grant Managua a $2.2 million loan to complete a road-building programme. One senior official, James Conrow, admitted that no loans to the Sandinistas would be supported 'until there are some fundamental changes in their policy.'

Of all aid entering Nicaragua, some 72% is from bilateral sources. The West provides 50% of this figure: the balance comes from the 'socialist bloc'. Many European countries have responded well to the current financial crisis - for example, Greece, Italy and France. Both France and Italy have extended new credit lines and sent valuable medical supplies. In the case of Italy, the new credit line is worth $40 million. Even West Germany provides small quantities of aid. Not as small, however, as those provided by Britain. According to the official HMG publication 'British Overseas Aid', **British aid to Nicaragua in 1982 totalled £49,000.** In comparison, British aid to the Turks and Caicos Islands was £5,716,000; to Paraguay £3,263,000; and to Honduras £1,072,000.

Military and Milicia

It has been put to us that there are over 100,000 people in Nicaragua with access to arms. In the view of the Deputy Foreign Minister of El Salvador, these constitute a Nicaraguan 'army'. We do not share that view. It is quite clear that the overwhelming majority of those with access to arms are local milicias - people in the main wanting to lead normal lives, and still doing normal work, who nonetheless are prepared to undergo a minimum of military training and put themselves at risk in defence of 'their' revolution.

We met members of both the army and the milicia during our stay in Nicaragua. We were accompanied to the border post of El Espino by two members of the regular army, and impressed by their coolness and professionalism on the outbreak of small arms fire. Both stressed that they were 'veterans' and both had action experience in the overthrow of Somoza and thereafter in operations countering the Contras. It became clear to us that this meant that they had been carrying arms and had been involved in military operations in their early teens. This is not surprising in a country where half the population is under the age of 16, although the nominal entry age for the milicia is 16 years.

It is clear to us that any invading force, whether Contras or a foreign power, would meet very considerable resistance in Nicaragua. Morale seemed very high among those we met. A major military operation involving US forces clearly could take certain points and probably some urban centres within the country. It is not clear to us that it could do much more. With over 100,000 people trained and with access to arms, and when even young people have become veterans through their experience against the Contras, not only the Somocista forces but also any invading power would be likely to face unacceptable losses if it attempted an invasion of the country.

It has been put to us that the CIA evaluates between 10,000 and 20,000 casualties (killed or wounded) in the event of an invasion of Nicaragua. The casualties on the other side would be tragic, but we find this estimate altogether plausible.

We did not discuss military strategy in the event of an invasion with the Nicaraguan authorities, but it is evident to us from other sources that while some of the main centres (including airports) would be strenuously defended, **the strategy of defence would amount to a major guerrilla operation in reclaiming their own country.** Strategic stockpiles of food and materiel have already been distributed.

We are struck in this respect by the geography of Nicaragua, its mountainous North-Western region, and the jungle of the Eastern half of the country. If the United States were to invade and hold some centres, it would then find itself subject to much the same scenario as in Vietnam. **There is no way in which the US would be likely to mobilise a popular resistance against the Sandinista government.** Indeed, an invasion could repeat the Bay of Pigs disaster on a more cataclysmic and more traumatic scale.

Bays in the geographic sense are relevant in such analysis, since it was put to us by Nicaraguan authorities that if the United States were to intervene with ground forces in El Salvador after the elections of 25th March, this certainly would include the Gulf of Fonseca between the two countries. In our own view this would be a pyrrhic occupation.

In political terms, we are persuaded that an invasion of Nicaragua would appall both international opinion and a broad section of public opinion in the United States, and prove little short of suicide for the administration concerned. This is for the Nicaraguans the best guarantee against such an invasion particularly in a US Presidential year.

It is partly for these reasons that we have argued earlier that **the Grenada example is misleading for Nicaragua and Central America** as a whole. Grenada is a very small country, which lacked an organised popular army to resist invasion. Nicaragua is a relatively large country, with a combination of both professional armed forces and milicia, well suited to effective guerrilla warfare. While it is possible that the Reagan administration reckoned that a quick feint on Grenada could be followed by the real punch on Nicaragua, the deterioration in El Salvador has landed it with the prospect of needing to deploy US ground troops there simply to hold the stalemate in that smaller, more populous country, much less suited to guerrilla warfare than Nicaragua.

It is also incredible to us that it should be claimed that Nicaragua aims to invade and occupy either Honduras or El Salvador. For one thing, it lacks the essential means of modern warfare necessary to effect such invasion, i.e. a combined armoured and air power. It has been reported to us from independent sources that the Nicaraguans may well have certain T54 tanks. But these are obsolete by any modern standards. It is the Honduran air force which dominates air power in the region, with not only super-mysteres but also several dozen other supersonic fighter aircraft. To our knowledge Nicaragua has no supersonic fighter or fighter-bomber aircraft available or deployed. There are only some two dozen or so helicopters available in the country. It is open to question whether it has deployed any ground-to-air missiles, and its air defences appear to be vintage ack-ack ground-to-air cannon.

In other words, in the lack of any convincing evidence produced elsewhere by the United States or other authorities, we are persuaded that **the deployment of the Nicaraguan military and militia is defensive rather than offensive.**

Peace Negotiations

We took extensive evidence on these matters from the Contadora ambassadors to Nicaragua. Stressing that the Contadora initiative depended essentially on mutual goodwill, and that the United States was not directly involved rather than consulted, the ambassadors also claimed that the question of negotiations on the security of the region could not be isolated from its underlying economic problems and the long-standing background of dictatorship and lack of democracy.

As one of them put it to us **'it is the IMF and the debt factor which is destabilising Latin American countries who cannot fulfil the most basic economic objectives.'** The Central American countries have debts of $14 billion on which they cannot even pay the interest. They lack oil, despite the credit lines from Colombia and Mexico. Costa Rica is effectively bankrupt.

Further, the collapse of the Central American Common Market - following both the war between Honduras and El Salvador and the revolution in Nicaragua - has reduced the viability of the traditional development model. Political problems block both road and sea transport, and mutual trade in the area.

According to the Contadora ambassadors, it is only after the main objective of avoiding war in the region has been achieved that it will be able to begin the massive problem of tackling these economic issues. We draw attention to the ratio of the scale of the long-term debt - at $14 billions, more than two-thirds of the maximum long-term aid for the region anticipated by the Kissinger Commission, and nearly double that recommended by the Commission for the period up to 1990.

The Nicaraguan Proposals

We secured copies of the Spanish text of 'Fundamental Commitments to Establish Peace in Central America' (the official Nicaraguan proposal within the framework of the Contadora process). Published in Managua on the 1st December 1983, these are the proposals which were considered and mainly welcomed by the Contadora ambassadors at their meeting of 20-21st December.

The Contadoran ambassadors commented on the substance of the proposals, which break down broadly into four areas:

(1) recognition of the basic principles of international law;

(2) restriction of arms and military expansion in the region;

(3) domestic politics and the international conditions for their autonomy;

(4) economic and social devlopment.

Stressing the principle of non-intervention in the region, the Nicaraguan proposals argue for a peaceful solution to differences and renunciation of recourse to force in the region; they also stress the importance of respect for the territorial integrity of states, pluralism in its various forms, democratic institutions, the promotion of social justice and human rights, international cooperation and development and proscription of terrorism and subversion.

It seems to us clear that − by whatever path and through whatever experience − the Nicaraguan government now is prepared to undertake commitments which avoid mutual subversion within the Central American region. For instance, in draft article 6 of the proposed treaty between Nicaragua and Honduras, the Nicaraguans propose that 'in the case that third countries declare war or undertake warlike actions against any of the two signatories, both agree without qualification not to undertake offensive alliances nor to request any kind of help or support from the enemies of either of the two republics'. Similarly article 9 of the same draft treaty proposed that 'in the case of circumstances or controversy between the two states which affect or could affect international peace and security, the signatories will recourse in the first instance to direct agreements, including the constitution of 'mixed' commissions to work towards their solution. If it is not possible to reach an agreement, they will take recourse to other means for the peaceful solution of differences recognised in Resolution 530 of the Security Council of the United Nations .. '

It is notable also that article 3 in the draft treaty between Nicaragua and the United States proposes that 'the signatory parties undertake not to give political, military, economic or any other form of aid, direct or indirect, open or covert, to individuals or groups who promote the undermining and destabilisation of the other government.' Article 7 proposes that 'the signatory parties solemnly undertake not to intervene, either directly or indirectly, openly or covertly, for whatever motive, in the internal and external affairs of the other state'.

We strongly recommend the detail and import of these proposals to international opinion.

PART SIX - FINDINGS AND RECOMMENDATIONS

The main range of our findings and recommendations have already been made explicit in the text of this report. In summary they include the following.

1. That the problems of the Central American Region are essentially North-South rather than East-West.

2. That Nicaragua poses no strategic threat to the United States, and denies military bases to the Soviet Union.

3. That the political security and autonomy of the Central American region can best be achieved by progress towards effective non-alignment.

4. That progressive demilitarisation of the region, including the withdrawal of the forces of any super power, or their surrogates, is both desirable and feasible, and could be supervised by the United Nations.

5. Any peace negotiated within the Central American region must respect the autonomy and independence of its sovereign states and peoples.

6. That attempts to isolate, strangle or suffocate individual countries in the Region by a combination of political, economic and military means are difficult in practice and would be profoundly damaging in principle even for a super power.

7. That there is no short-term military solution in El Salvador, and that a political solution cannot be achieved simply by the holding of elections on the

25th March, not least if this results in the election of the 'pathological killer' d'Aubuisson.

8. That granted polarisation and the lack of a 'middle ground' in El Salvador, progress towards a political and military solution can only achieved by negotiating the main four demands of the FDR-FMLN.

9. That in terms of international law there is no essential difference between the direct invasion of Grenada and the indirect invasion of Nicaragua by a United States-trained and financed Contra force.

10 That the moral authority of the United States in international organisations — for instance to criticise the Soviet invasion of Afghanistan — is undermined by their support for Contra actions based from Honduras against Nicaragua and that the United States should cease overt or cover support to the military enemies of Nicaragua.

11. That the United States and Honduras should be urged to respond to the proposals for bi-lateral treaties with Nicaragua made on 1st December 1983 by the Nicaragua government within the framework of Contadora.

12. That the United States should show the same concern for land reform, and economic development in Honduras that it at present prioritises in El Salvador, and that a new model of development could well be achieved in the region, provided that its export markets are diversified, and that multilateral aid is freed from IMF-type 'conditionality'.

13. That the vast expenditure of economic assistance recommended by the Kissinger Commission is likely to profit bank

accounts in Miami unless political and economic structures for its absorption are reformed in individual countries.

14. That the funds of the new Central American Development Organisation should be scheduled on neutral and objective criteria to the Central American economies, possibly based on a combined need and resources index of total population and Gross Domestic Product per head.

15. That the long-term economic aid proposals recommended by the Kissinger Report will not be achieved, and that economic aid in the short term will be allocated to El Salvador and Honduras as instruments of counter-insurgency rather than economic development.

16. That multilateral agencies including the International Monetary Fund and the World Bank should restore their aid to Nicaragua at least to levels comparable with their aid to neighbouring countries.

17. That individual governments such as that of the United Kingdom, which has dramatically cut its aid programme to Nicaragua while raising it in other areas (including a doubling of aid to Grenada) should similarly restore their aid programme.

18. That in the event of the World Bank, the IMF and the Inter-American Development Bank failing to restore aid to Nicaragua this should be offset by a combination of multilateral and bilateral aid from other countries - including those in Western Europe.

19. That in the event of European governments including those within the European Economic Community failing to realise a higher level of economic

assistance to Nicaragua, the governments within the Socialist International should be encouraged to increase their aid.

20. That if the United Kindgom government is not simply to echo the judgement of the United States in the Central American region, it should improve its representation, including the establishment of resident diplomatic representation in Managua and San Salvador.

21. That the specific proposals of the Hague Conference and Initiative of June 1983 should be strongly endorsed by governments concerned for the political and economic autonomy of the Central American region.

22. That support should be encouraged for the declaration of the Trans-National Institute with regard to the independence, sovereign rights and economic autonomy of the region.

Never Kneel Down: Drought, development and liberation in Eritrea

by Stuart Holland and James Firebrace, with an introduction by Neil Kinnock

The war in Eritrea is now in its twenty-third year. Hundreds of thousands have been killed or disabled or have fled their homes. Over a third of the population is now facing a major famine. Africa's longest liberation struggle has been fought against successive Ethiopian regimes, backed and heavily armed first by the USA and now by the USSR. The Eritrean People's Liberation Front, who administer 80 per cent of the Eritrean countryside, are now winning major victories which may prove to be the turning point of this war. The EPLF have not only been fighting for Eritrea's right to self-determination, but also for the transformation of traditional social structures which have served to perpetuate poverty, famine and oppression. They have introduced land reforms, have established a network of services providing the population with basic health care and education, and have implemented practical measures to ensure women's rights, denied to them in feudal society.

This book is a result of a fact-finding mission made by Stuart Holland MP, Labour Shadow Minister for Overseas Development, and James Firebrace, War on Want's Programme Officer for the Horn of Africa. It makes recommendations on how concerned parties and movements in Europe can play an increasingly important role in the search for a just solution to the conflict. The book includes a series of photographs and maps.

Cloth £12.00   Paper £3.95

SPOKESMAN

Bertrand Russell House, Gamble Street, Nottingham NG7 4ET
England.

Books on regular loan may be checked out for **two weeks**. Books must be presented at the Circulation Desk in order to be renewed.

A fine is charged after date due.

Special books are subject to special regulations at the discretion of the library staff.

MAR. 23.1968			